Gliding

by Ann Welch

produced in collaboration with the
British Gliding Association

Published by A & C Black (Publishers) Ltd
35 Bedford Row, London WC1R 4JH

CONTENTS

Front cover shows an ASTIR competition glider flown by J. Trzeciak from Poland, crossing the finish line at Rieti, Italy.
Photographs and drawings by Ann Welch.

INTRODUCTION

Gliding is the challenge and fun of flying without an engine, using only your skill and the invisible energy that is in the air. It all started a long time ago with man's early dreams to fly like the birds, but achievement only came slowly. The first really successful pilot was Otto Lilienthal. 95 years ago he built not only several gliders but also a hill in Germany from which to launch himself! Altogether he made over 2,000 flights. At much the same time, the English pilot Percy Pilcher was flying his own gliders in Kent.

Following the invention of the aeroplane in 1903 not much happened for a while until Pelzner and others in Germany started experiments with simple gliders in the Rhön mountains around 1912. Ten years after that two pilots, Klemperer and Martens, built and flew their gliders – the Schwarzer Teufel and Vampyr – which led the way to the sport as we know it today. They learned to soar over the hills, but the use of thermal upcurrents under cumulus clouds did not follow for almost another decade. Robert Kronfeld and Wolf Hirth were the famous pioneers of thermal soaring away from the hills.

The first big gliding event in Britain was at Itford, Sussex, in 1922, with a competition for duration soaring organised by the *Daily Mail*. It was won by the French pilot, Maneyrol, with a flight of 3 hrs 21 mins. By the early 1930s gliding clubs were springing up all over the country, and the British Gliding Association was formed. The most important club of the early days was the London Gliding Club at Dunstable. During this period cross-country soaring using thermal upcurrents developed rapidly, the world distance record going from 164 km in 1930 to 750 km in 1939. Most British records at this time were held by Philip Wills.

Over the last 35 years the accent has been on speed flying – to design gliders which will fly fast and so make the best use of the limited hours of soaring that are possible in a day. In good weather gliders now soar cross-country faster than many light aeroplanes. The skills needed to fly these superb gliders really well are great, but that pilot ability has kept pace with glider design is shown by the results of world championships and records. The longest distance flown is now more than 1000 miles and the fastest speed around a triangular course is 195 km per hour.

Most glider pilots do not aspire to such great things but enjoy their gliding no less. Every fine summer weekend in Britain hundreds of gliders are flying, largely unnoticed because they are so quiet. There is nothing else that their pilots would rather be doing.

Note on Units

Gliding uses a mixture of units; kilometres for distances, knots (nautical miles per hour) for speeds, and the international aeronautical unit for height – feet. Weights are now generally metric. All these units have been used in this book, but to help the reader conversions to kilometres per hour or feet per minute have been added after figures in knots.

Milestones in World Gliding

Sir George Cayley made the first known glider flight in 1853. The pilot was his coachman, and the flight ended in a hedge.

Otto Lilienthal had made 2000 flights by 1896, many from a home-built hill. He was the forerunner of hang gliding.

Hans Gutermuth in 1911 flew 1000 m in a home-built hang glider from the Wasserkuppe.

Wolfgang Klemperer was the first to fly 5 km in 1921 in his Blaue Maus.

Max Kegel in 1926 made the first distance flight in a thunderstorm. He flew 55 km from the Wasserkuppe.

Wolf Hirth in 1934 was the first to soar 300 km in his Moazagotl from the Wasserkuppe to Goerlitz.

R. Oelszschner, O. Brautigam, E. Steinhoff and Heinemann all flew the first 500 km distance in 1935, from the Wasserkuppe to Brno in Czechoslovakia.

Geoffrey Stephenson was the first pilot to soar across the English Channel on 22 April 1938 in his Slingsby Gull.

Sigi Maurer in July 1948 established the first 100 km triangle record of 69.6 km/h in Switzerland in a Moswey.

Al Parker, in 1964, was the first to fly a distance of more than 1000 km. He flew from Odessa, Texas, to Kimball, Nebraska, taking 10½ hours in his Sisu.

Paul Bikle in 1961 reached the greatest height ever—14,102 m—in a Schweizer 1–23 from Bishop, California.

Hans Werner Grosse in 1977 was the first to fly around a 1000 km triangle in Australia in his ASW–17 at a speed of 98.5 km/h.

Karl Striedeck achieved the first 1000 mile flight in 1976 as an out-and-return along the Appalachian mountains, but his barograph did not work so he made the same flight again in 1977.

HOW A GLIDER FLIES

Because a glider is heavier than air it will only fly when its wing provides enough lift to support its weight. To generate this lift the glider has to travel through the air with sufficient speed. The necessary speed is obtained by gravity. The glider has to fly downhill through the air all the time – much as a cyclist maintains his speed freewheeling downhill. If the pilot flies too slowly the wing will stall – rather as the cyclist will topple off. The glide slope necessary to maintain flying speed is made as flat as possible. A top competition glider has a glide ratio of about 55:1. This means that in still air it can glide a theoretical 55 nautical miles from a height of 1 nautical mile or 6,080 ft. A school glider has a glide ratio of about 25:1 or 30:1. The sinking speed of a glider is the *rate* at which it loses height while gliding down, typically about 150 feet per minute.

The best gliding angle is achieved only when the glider is being flown at the speed which gives the best relationship of lift to drag (the resistance of the glider to its passage through the air). This speed is usually about 45 knots (83km per hour), or 10 knots above the stalling speed. If the best lift to drag, or L/D, speed is exceeded the glider will be diving off height and the glide slope will be steeper. If the glider is flown slower than the best L/D speed – at only a few knots above the stalling speed – drag is higher, worsening the glide slope. However, because of the lower flying speed the rate of sink may be at its lowest in spite of the slightly steeper gliding angle.

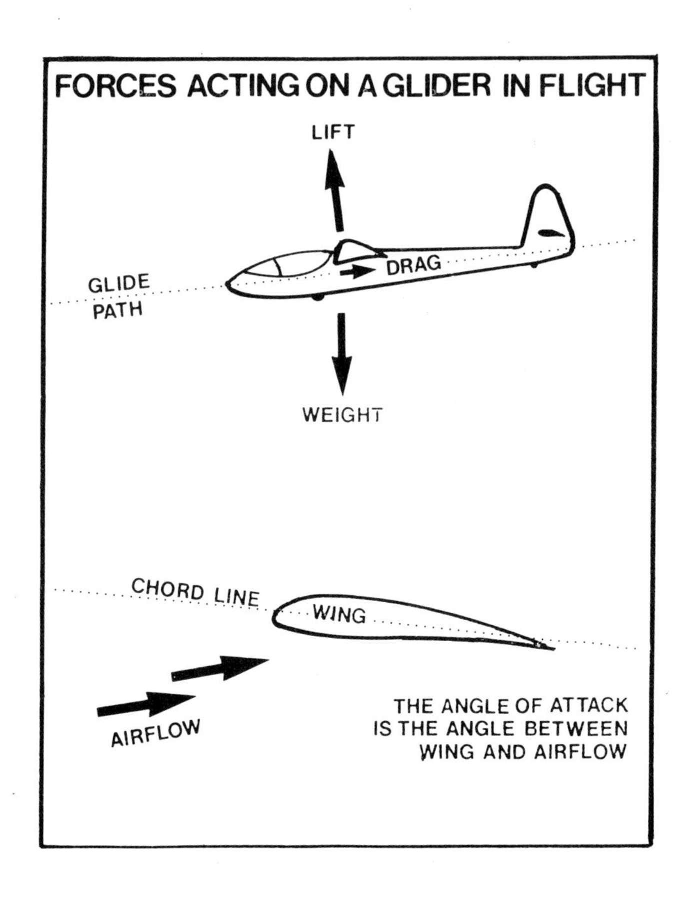

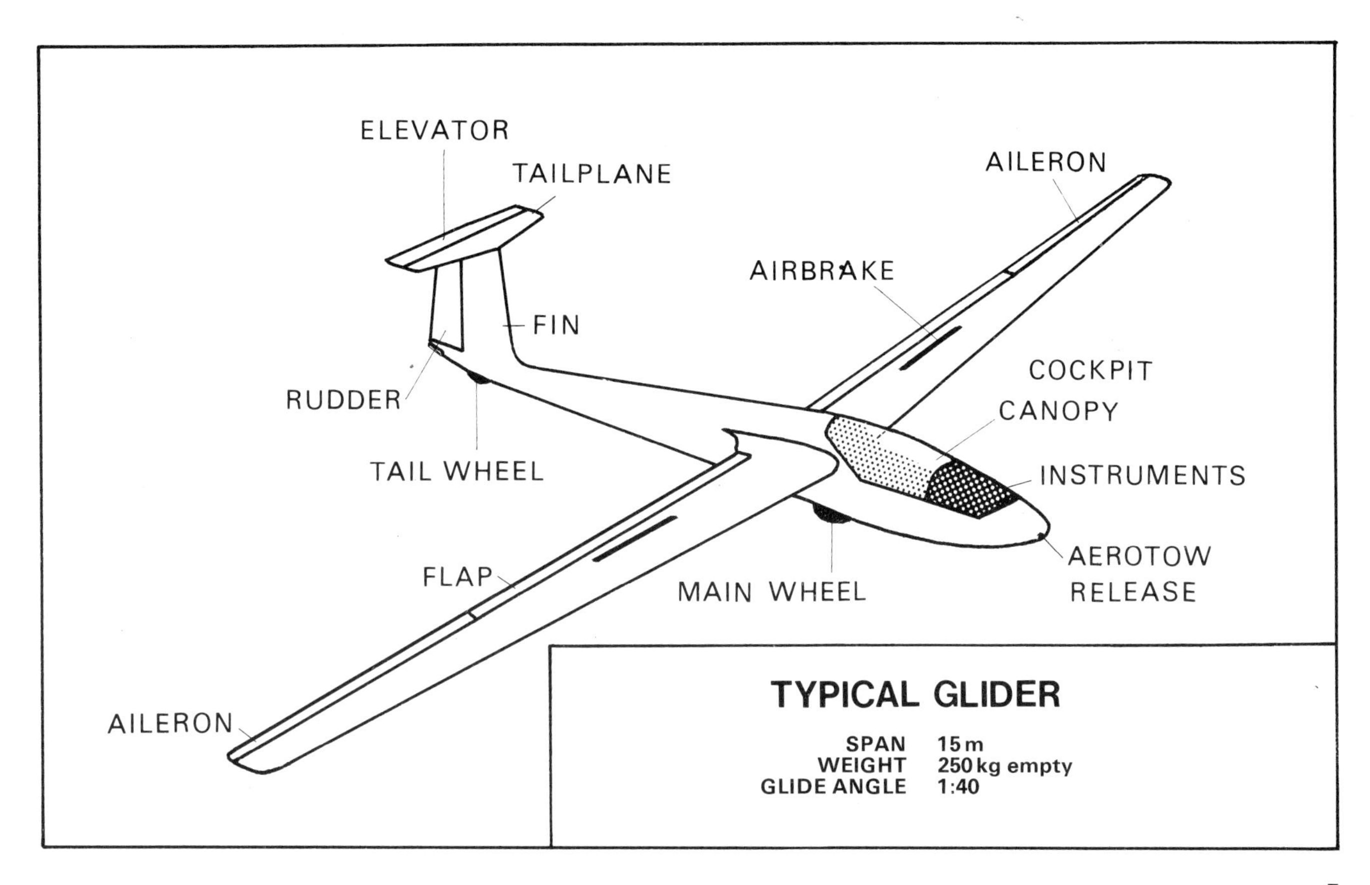

TYPICAL GLIDER

SPAN	**15 m**
WEIGHT	**250 kg empty**
GLIDE ANGLE	**1:40**

The skilled pilot uses the relationship between speed, glide ratio and sink rate with great accuracy to make his glider go as far or as fast as possible when soaring.

To obtain high performance the wing of the glider is long and narrow. The wing span may be between 15 and 24 metres, and the aspect ratio (ratio of span to width of the wing) 25 or over. The wing section, or profile, is designed to obtain a smooth airflow over much of the surface of the wing, and the surface finish has to be superbly smooth.

Size, Weight, etc.

Traditionally gliders were made of wood, usually spruce, and birch plywood. Some gliders are made of metal, such as welded steel tube or aluminium, but most modern gliders are now made of glass fibre. This material is not only strong but makes possible the smooth finish necessary for high performance. School gliders are still more often made of wood, or have wood wings and a steel tube fuselage.

The empty weight of gliders ranges from 200 kg for a club single seater to 350 kg for a school two seater, or a glass fibre competition single seater of 20 m span. Apart from trainers nearly all gliders are single seaters, because soaring is essentially a solo endeavour.

Although gliders do not weigh very much they are designed to be strong enough to be flown in conditions of great turbulence such as are found over mountains or inside thunderstorms.

Student, instructor and 2 seater

Pilot with parachute getting into the cockpit

The Cockpit

To reduce the drag the glider cockpit is made with as small a cross-section as will permit the pilot to fly efficiently and safely. In high performance gliders the pilot is in a reclining, comfortable position with the canopy only a few centimetres above his head. Sometimes the canopy can mist up, so a sliding clear vision panel is fitted. The seat is designed for a pilot wearing a slim back-type parachute, and there is a harness to hold him comfortably in place in rough air.

The Controls

The control stick is between the pilot's knees. The rudder pedals are often adjustable. On the left of the cockpit are the airbrake and/or flap controls, and the yellow knob which is pulled to release the launching cable. Most gliders are fitted with a trimmer lever. The trimmer adjusts the fore and aft loads on the stick by means of either a spring in the elevator circuit or a tab on the elevator itself. There may also be a retraction lever for raising the main wheel.

Instruments

There are three basic flight instruments:

The **airspeed indicator** gives the speed of the glider *through the air*, usually in knots (nautical miles per hour). It does not indicate the speed that the glider is travelling over the ground, except when there is absolutely no wind.

The **altimeter** indicates the height of the glider. It is simply a barometer giving the air pressure presented on an instrument dial in terms of altitude. If the altimeter is set to zero before take-off it will indicate height above the airfield when in the air. Alternatively it can be set at airfield elevation and in the air will then give readings of altitude above sea level. This setting is used for cross-country soaring. Because the altimeter is a barometer its altitude indications will alter as the outside air pressure changes, so if the pressure on the ground decreases the altimeter will show altitude that the pilot has not got. For this reason a corrected pressure setting is used if the pilot wants to know his altitude precisely.

The **variometer** shows the pilot when his glider is rising and gaining height, and when it is going down. In air without upcurrents or downcurrents the variometer of a glider flying at a steady speed will show the sink rate performance of the glider. When it is flown into an upcurrent the variometer will show the net rate of rise. It operates on the pressure difference between the outside air and that in a capacity flask or air storage container; the outside air pressure lessens as the glider rises and air in the flask will flow out causing movement of the dial needle.

Electric variometers operate by measuring the cooling effect of the air on small electric elements as it flows into or out of the capacity flask. Although more expensive they are preferred by many competition pilots because they are more sensitive. Variometers are often fitted with a 'speed-to-fly', or MacCready, ring.

Instrument Panel

When adjusted according to the strength of the upcurrents being used, it tells the pilot at what speed he should fly between thermals to obtain the fastest cross-country speed.

The instrument panel may also carry an **artificial horizon** and/or a **turn–and–slip indicator** for cloud flying, and a **compass**.

How the Controls Work

The pilot controls his glider by means of small movable surfaces on the wings and tail. These are connected to his control stick and rudder pedals, as in any other aircraft.

Control in pitch – nose down to increase speed and nose up to reduce speed – is obtained by fore and aft movements of the stick which moves the elevator down and up. Control in roll – banking in order to turn – is obtained by lateral movements of the same stick which moves the ailerons. Moving the stick to the left, for example, will bank the glider to the left. The rudder pedals produce skid, or yaw; pressing the left foot yaws the nose of the glider to the left. A turn is made using both ailerons and rudder at the same time. The controls of a glider are quite sensitive and only small light movements are necessary.

Almost all gliders have airbrakes. These are vertical surfaces designed into the wing which, when raised, will produce a lot of drag. Without them, the flat gliding angle would make landing in a field, or even on an airfield, very difficult. Opening the airbrakes increases the drag of the glider so that it descends more steeply, and to maintain the same speed the pilot has to lower the nose. This steeper approach path can be adjusted by varying the amount of airbrake used to enable the pilot to land at the intended place.

Some gliders are fitted with flaps. These are normally used to make slight alterations to the shape of the wing section to modify its slow- or high-speed performance. If the flaps are raised slightly above neutral the highspeed performance will be improved, but the glider will not fly so well at low speeds. With the flaps lowered a few degrees the wing will provide more lift for slow flight, but also more drag. Some flaps have been designed to be lowered to 85°–90° and they then produce enough drag to be used as airbrakes.

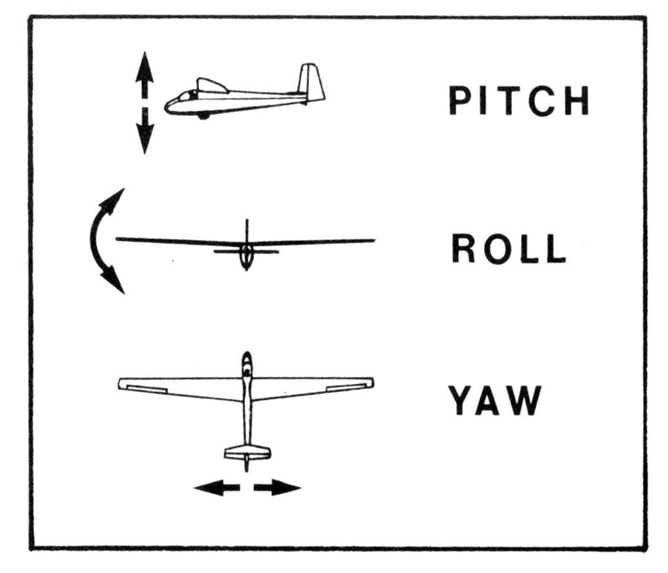

LAUNCHING

Methods

Gliders are launched into the air by towing them with an aeroplane or a car, by winch, or occasionally by a rubber shock cord catapult. Launches are usually made facing into wind.

The advantage of aerotowing is that the glider can be taken to, and released in, an area of lift. It may also be retrieved following an away landing if the field is large enough. Most light aeroplanes with an engine of 130 hp or more are suitable; they have a release attachment fitted at the tail. The tow rope is usually nylon, about 40–50 metres long, with a breaking load of 454 kg. The glider is usually towed to a height of 2,000 ft., at which height the glider pilot releases his end of the rope. In an emergency, such as loss of engine power, the tug pilot will rock his wings. This is an order to the glider pilot to release and it must be obeyed. If it is not, the tug pilot will let go his end of the rope.

Car launching is practicable if the airfield has a runway. The towcar is attached to the glider by a wire cable about 400 metres long. The car drives at a fast enough speed for the glider to fly. At a safe height – about 100 ft. – the glider pilot is able to climb more steeply, kiting up on the wire to about 1,000 ft., sometimes more. When the car nears the end of the runway and decelerates, the pilot releases his end of the cable, which falls to the ground slowed by a small parachute.

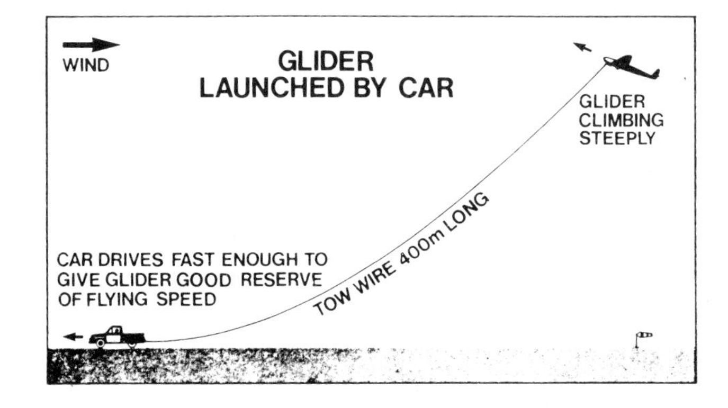

A winch launch is similar to a car tow except that the winch is stationary, and the engine power is used to wind in the cable at high speed onto a drum. Winch launching is used where the surface is unsuitable for towing. After the launch the cable is retrieved and towed back to the launch point. If the ground is very rough this may have to be done by a tractor. Some winches are built with two drums so that the cables are retrieved only after every second launch.

In the past much soaring was done from hills, and gliders were catapulted off the hilltop by means of a rubber rope stretched out in a V by half a dozen people. This method is still in use if the site and wind are suitable and the glider is not too heavy or fast.

The Release

The cable release mechanism is normally fitted with an automatic back-releasing device. Should the pilot forget or be unable to release the cable and overfly the winch or tow car the now-backward pull of the cable on the mechanism will cause the release to open and the cable end to fall out. Some gliders have two releases, one aft under the cockpit for steep car or winch launches, and one in the nose for aerotowing. For catapult launches the glider can use a simple open hook, the shock cord falling off when it is no longer under tension.

About 10 launches an hour are usual with a tow car, about 6 with aerotowing, and 8 with winch launching.

Ready for Take-Off

When the pilot is ready to take off, the launching cable or tow rope is attached to the quick-release hook under the nose of the glider; the crewman calls 'Open', inserts the linked ring, and then calls 'Close' to the pilot. The wings are held level by the wingtip holder who prepares to run when the launch commences.

Helper running at wingtip

Another person signals to the winch or tug aeroplane, usually with a bat, but before doing so must look around to see that no other aircraft are about to land and that there are no obstructions in the way of the launch. At the pilot's request he signals for the slack in the cable to be taken up. When it is taut the pilot calls 'All Out' to the signaller. Full power is applied and the glider takes off. If anything is thought to be wrong at the start of the launch the signal for 'Stop' can be given by anyone present who considers that all is not well – such as if the glider overruns the end of the cable with the possible risk of it catching round the landing wheel or skid. The three signals are shown below.

Take up slack

All Out

Stop

LEARNING TO FLY

Anyone aged 16 or over may fly a glider provided he or she is able to sign a Declaration of Physical Fitness. Gliding in Britain takes place in clubs which provide training for would-be pilots. Instructors are qualified by the British Gliding Association, and most of them are voluntary. Learning to fly is best accomplished by starting on a course of 1 or 2 weeks' duration, but many people are unable to get to their club except at weekends. If lessons are separated by more than a week learning to fly can be a slow process.

Having joined a club, the new pilot will discover that the more he is willing to help with getting gliders out to the launch point, keeping the flight log sheet, running at wingtips, and pushing gliders back after landing, the more flying he will get. To speed up learning, some clubs use a 2-seat motor glider for the basic lessons. The instructor and student take off when ready, and the lesson can be tailored to the weather. The student converts to 2-seat gliders after about $3\frac{1}{2}$ hours flying on the motor glider and before he flies solo. If he learns completely on gliders he will need an average of about 60 winch launches before flying solo.

Moving a glider to the launch point

Clothing and health

Gliding fields can be cold even in summer, so warm, windproof clothes are needed. Footwear should be comfortable and suitable for wet grass and, on some sites, rough ground.

A pilot should not fly if he does not feel well, has a cold or earache, or is taking medication. If in doubt he should obtain advice from a doctor.

It is natural that the student pilot should feel tired after long hours out at the launch point. Chocolate or sweets help.

Ground Handling

The first lesson will be to learn how to handle gliders on the ground and to park them so that they will not be damaged or blown over. A glider should be held or pushed only on the nose or the leading edge of the wing, and held level only at the wingtip. It should always be parked turned across wind, with the windward wing weighted down with a tyre and the wheel blocked.

The Cockpit Check

Every day, before flying, the glider has to be inspected for wear and tear and possible damage. In addition, before every take-off the pilot should carry out a cockpit check. The standard check list is memorised by the initials CBSIFTCB.

C Controls	Do the stick and rudder pedals move correctly, fully and freely, not obstructed by cushions, cameras, etc.?
B Ballast	Is the weight correct? A glider can only be flown safely if the load in the cockpit – the pilot(s) and equipment – is within the limits stated on the flight limitations label. This must be checked and ballast added if the pilot does not weigh enough.
S Straps	Are the harness straps of both instructor and student fastened correctly and firmly?
I Instruments	Are the instruments undamaged and is the altimeter set correctly?
F Flaps (if fitted)	Is the flap setting correct? They should be set for take-off.
T Trim	Does the trimmer lever move fully and freely? It should be positioned for take-off.
C Canopy	Is the canopy closed properly?
B Brakes	Are the airbrakes closed? In a strong wind it may be wise to leave the airbrakes open on the ground, but they must be closed and locked before take-off.

The glider is now ready for flight and to have the launching cable attached.

First Flights

The very first air experience flight will be made by the instructor who will explain what the glider is doing, how the controls are moved and point out the landing area and other landmarks. The student will be shown the controls, but will not be expected to fly himself. It is quite normal to feel some apprehension if you have not flown before, but once in the air on a nice day the delights of flying will quickly become apparent. From the second flight on, you will start to use the controls yourself under the direction of the instructor. You will soon discover that the glider is stable and that it needs only a light hand on the controls to guide it.

The first step is to learn to fly the glider at the right speed and attitude. This will be about 40 knots (74 km per hour) with the nose about a handspan below the horizon, as demonstrated by the instructor. See A in the diagram. If the speed increases (C) the stick is gently moved back to raise the nose, and if the speed becomes slower than it should (B) the nose is lowered until the attitude is again correct. At the same time the wings have to be kept level so that the glider will fly straight. Only small control movements are needed and the stick should be held lightly. From the start the new pilot must keep a good lookout for other aircraft.

At first there seems too much to do at the same time, and you are likely to find good co-ordination of the controls harder than you expected. Don't despair; usually a little steady practice is all that is needed.

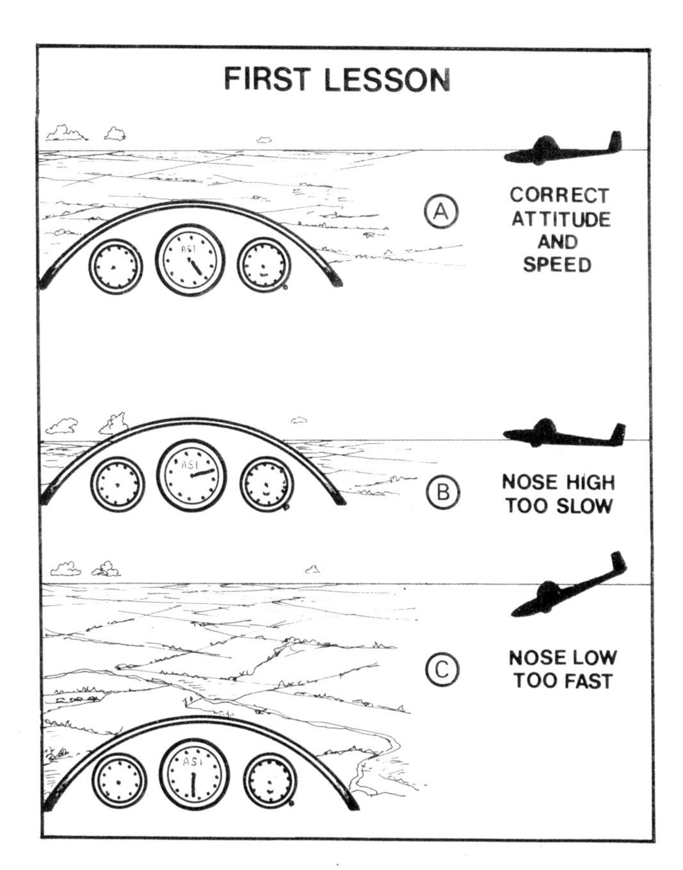

Turning

Turns are made by banking the glider – about 30°–35° for a medium turn, together with some rudder. When the glider is in the turn little or no rudder will be found to be necessary, and the desired bank should be maintained by use of aileron control. The speed should be kept steady. To stop the turn and again fly straight, the wings should be levelled by using aileron and rudder together to come smoothly out of the turn. Speed should be re-checked. If a turn is made with too much rudder for the chosen angle of bank the glider will skid outwards during the turn. With insufficient rudder, it will slip inwards. Both faults will feel uncomfortable, will increase drag, and spoil the glider's performance.

In a turn the stalling speed is increased because the glider carries the extra load imparted by centrifugal force. The increase is negligible in gentle or medium turns, but considerable at high angles of bank. Speed should therefore be increased before starting steep turns. During turns the noise should be prevented from going down, and the speed increasing, by some backward pressure on the stick. In steep turns a considerable amount of backward pressure will be needed to keep the nose up and travelling evenly around the horizon. A steep turn is difficult to do well and should the pilot feel he is not able to control it he should immediately take off bank, and reduce the rate of turn. Since the glider pilot will need to circle continuously and accurately in up-currents in order to soar, it is important that he learns properly to understand and control the turn.

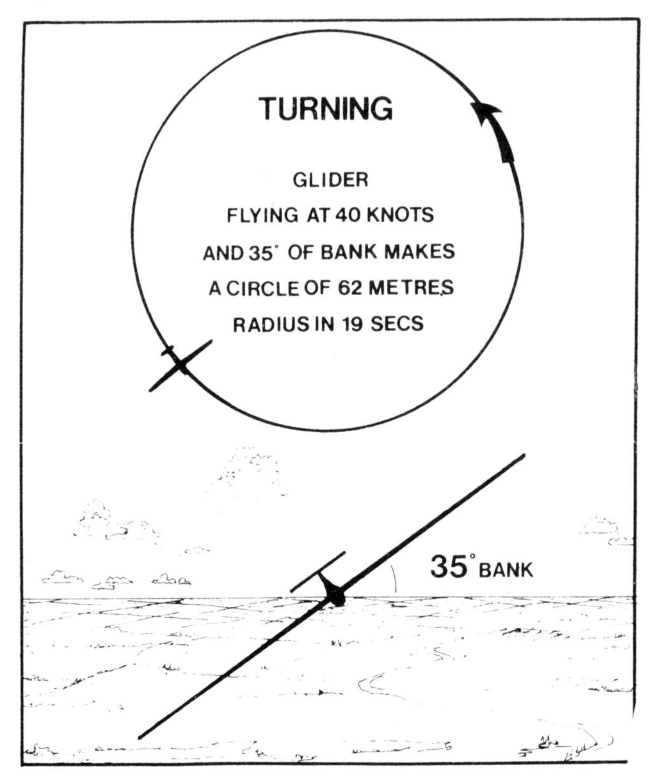

Take-Off

As soon as the student is able to handle the glider in the air he can learn to take off. When the cockpit check has been completed, signals are given for the launch to start. The glider is pulled forward, accelerating rapidly, and soon has flying speed. Before this stage, however, the wingtip runner has probably been outpaced, so the pilot himself must keep the wings level and the glider running straight, as well as allow it to become airborne in a level attitude. As soon as the glider is in the air it will want to climb steeply, and has to be restrained so that the climb angle is only gentle until the safe height of about 100 ft. is reached. The pilot should keep his left hand near the release so that if the cable breaks he can not only get the nose down quickly to maintain enough flying speed, but get rid of whatever is left of the trailing end of the cable. Above 100 ft. the pilot can and should climb the glider more steeply so as to gain height rapidly. Near the top of the launch the pull of the cable will be more directly from below and will start pulling the nose of the glider down nearer to the normal flying attitude. When the pilot feels the power fade he should lower the nose, release the cable, and then adjust the attitude to obtain normal flying speed.

Landing

A good landing is most easily made from a high straight approach made at the correct speed. The object is to gradually alter the path of the glider from a relatively steep glide slope so that when it arrives on the ground it will be in the landing attitude and near stall speed. If the round out – or flare – is made too high the glider will subsequently sink heavily, partially stalled, onto the ground. If made too low, it will hit on its landing wheel and bounce, because it still has flying speed. As he gets closer to the ground, the pilot should look well ahead and try to judge the rate at which he must adjust his glide path by gently easing back on the stick. The glider should touch down on its main wheel and tail skid at the same time. It must then be kept running straight with the wings held level until it stops, when one wing will subside gently onto the ground.

Airbrakes

The next step is to learn to use the airbrakes to control the approach path so that the glider is landed precisely where the pilot intends. The approach should be made with a margin of extra speed – usually around 10 knots (20 km per hour) above the ordinary gliding speed in the air. When the airbrakes are opened the nose has to be lowered further to overcome the drag sufficiently to maintain a safe approach speed. The glider is now descending more steeply and if the brakes are held fully open during the landing, the glider will decelerate rapidly during the round-out. On the approach airbrakes should be used as an adjustment to maintain a steady rate of descent, the pilot moving them gently in and out as necessary. It is advisable, to begin with, to avoid moving the airbrakes during the landing round-out process, as it is easy to become muddled between the movements of the stick and the airbrake lever. After landing the airbrakes should be opened fully to reduce the landing run.

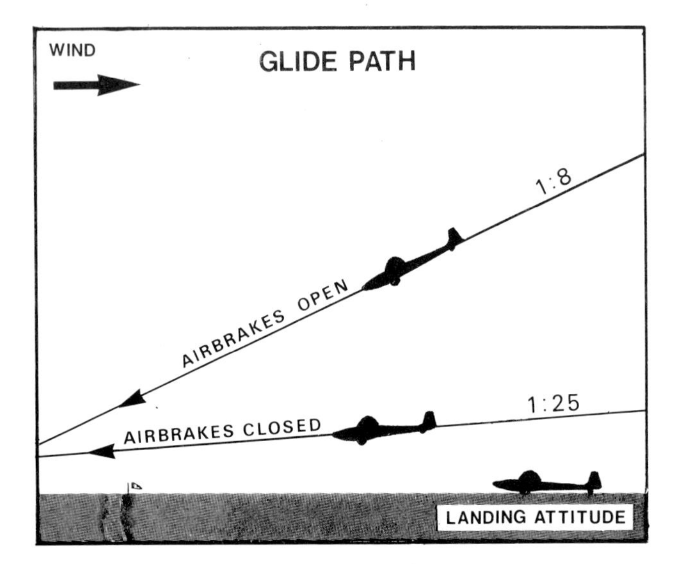

Planning the Approach to Land

From any given height the glider has to fly a path of a certain length before it will reach the ground. It is conventional, therefore, to use up this height by flying a partial circuit or pattern around the landing area. This not only reduces the risk of collision but enables the pilot to organise his position in the air so that he will have time to assess the wind direction and strength, to take any necessary actions such as lowering the landing gear; and then land where he wants.

The usual glider circuit pattern is achieved by starting from a point upwind and to one side of the landing field at a height of about 600 ft. The glider is then flown downwind until it is level with or a little behind the downwind boundary, depending on the wind strength. It is then turned across wind on to the base leg where finer adjustments in positioning can be carried out, and a further good search made for the whereabouts of other aircraft. The glider should now be flying at its higher approach speed, and the pilot should have his hand ready on the airbrake lever. When nearing the line of the final approach and landing the glider should be turned into wind, with airbrakes used as necessary to achieve the point where the pilot intends to land. If, during the downwind leg, the glider is still higher than expected, a slightly wider circuit should be flown, or airbrakes used earlier. If it is low, the glider should be turned in towards the landing area while it still has enough height to make the turn safely.

It is best to land the glider directly into wind, but often the wind will be blowing obliquely across the landing area. A cross wind will affect the whole circuit. On a normal circuit the downwind leg will be made at a higher groundspeed and on the base leg the glider will be drifted back, away from the landing area; it will have a slow speed over the ground on the final into-wind approach. When there is a cross wind the glider will be drifted into or away from the field on the 'downwind' leg, depending on the direction of the cross wind; it will be slowed down or speeded up over the ground on base leg, and will be drifted sideways across the ground during the final approach. Before landing, any sideways drift of the glider has to be corrected if the landing gear is not to be subjected to undue loads. This is best done by using rudder to swing the nose in the direction that the glider is drifting (downwind) immediately before touchdown. This allows the landing wheel to make contact with the ground without sideways drift.

The pilot of a high performance competition glider will start his approach lower than from 600 ft, so the student pilot must remember to keep a good look out below, as well as all around him.

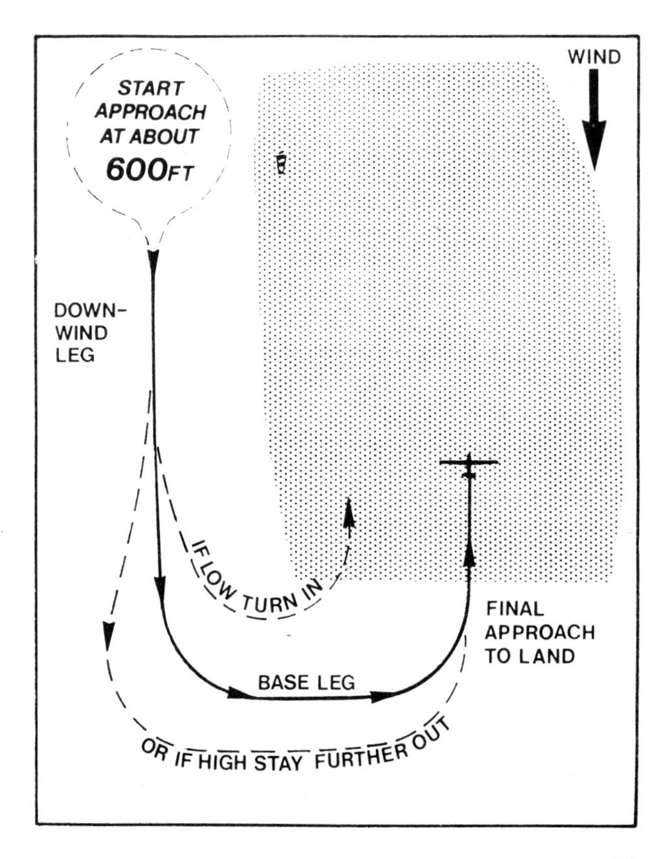

Emergency Procedure—Cable Breaks

Should the launch cable break, or the winch engine power fade, the pilot should deal with the situation in such a way that the glider will be landed safely. The first essentials are to maintain, or regain, enough speed and to get rid of the cable end. If the glider is still close to the ground – less than about 100 ft. up (see 'A' in the diagram) – it should be landed straight ahead; it may not be necessary, or practicable, to use the airbrakes. From greater heights (see 'B') landing ahead within the airfield may be impossible even with full airbrakes. In this case the glider should immediately be turned to one side. The direction in which this turn is made should take advantage of the wind and the shape of the field, so that when the glider is turned back again it will be more nearly into wind and/or will have the biggest clear area ahead. If the glider is still so high after the first turn to one side ('C') that it would not be possible to land anywhere ahead in the airfield, then the turn should be continued, and the glider flown around an abbreviated circuit.

With much less than the usual height no attempt should be made to return to the normal landing area. The glider should be turned into wind while it still has plenty of height, and landed well into the field.

If a rope breaks on aerotow, or if the glider pilot is waved off by the tug pilot, there may be no possibility of getting back into the airfield, and the glider pilot should fly ahead into the largest convenient field, using airbrakes as soon as he is sure that he will be able to cross the near hedge. Although the glider may not have much height in an aerotow emergency the speed of the tow will probably leave the glider pilot with some reserve in hand.

Simulated cable breaks and launch failures are given during training so that the pilot becomes familiar with the necessary safety procedures.

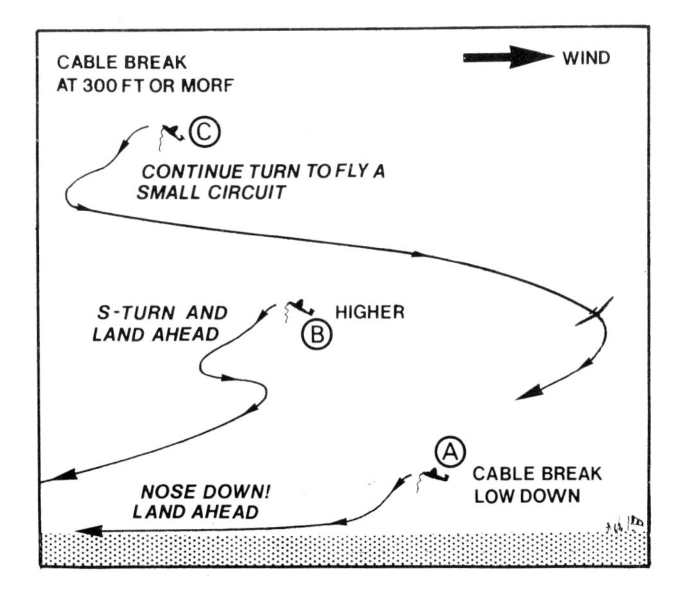

Emergency Procedure—Stalls and Spins

Unless a pilot is interested in aerobatics his intention is always to avoid stalling or spinning, but he has to learn about them so that he will know how to recover quickly should he ever inadvertently fly too slowly and stall. The symptoms of an approaching stall are a) airspeed indicator showing less than it should; b) nose higher than usual; c) less noise; d) sloppy feel to the controls, and e) sometimes buffeting due to the disturbed airflow over the partially stalled wing. If any of these symptoms are noticed the nose should be lowered and speed increased.

The Spin

A spin can only develop from a stalled condition in which one wing drops. In a turn the inner wing is flying through the air more slowly and with a greater angle of attack than the outer one; if the glider's speed is insufficient the inner wing will stall first and drop. This is the beginning of a spin. If the pilot checks it quickly enough by lowering the nose and keeping straight with rudder the wings will unstall, the incipient spin will be stopped and little height will be lost. If it is not checked the aircraft will start to rotate, spinning with its nose well down, and losing height quickly but not gaining speed. Considerable height will be lost before recovery can be made. This is why it is dangerous to fly slowly near the ground. To make sure of recovery from a spin the controls have to be moved in a certain manner. Full opposite rudder has to be applied, and after a pause the stick must be moved steadily forward until the spinning stops. The glider can then be returned to the normal flying attitude. Although the full recovery drill should always be initiated many gliders will stop spinning as soon as the pilot starts the recovery action.

If, during the recovery dive, speed becomes excessively high, the airbrakes should be opened. The most likely time for a pilot to spin by mistake is when he is low, concentrating on a difficult landing, and is distracted by drifting out of position, or by the proximity of other gliders, or sudden turbulence, and he allows the glider to stall in a turn. If he does not immediately recognise what is happening his instinctive actions – such as trying to raise the nose – will delay or prevent recovery.

Sometimes a spin changes into a spiral dive; this is recognisable because the airspeed indicator shows rapidly increasing speed instead of the low, constant speed of a spin. If speed rapidly increases, the pilot should open the airbrakes, take off bank, and *gently* pull out of the dive.

Rules of the Air

Before flying solo the pilot must know the rules of the air. These are:

Meeting head on

Each pilot must turn away to his right.

Converging

When two gliders are on converging courses, the glider which has the other on its right must give way. The pilot giving way may do so by diverging or by passing behind the other glider, whichever seems safer.

Overtaking

An aeroplane may only overtake by passing to the right of the aircraft being overtaken, but (in the U.K.) a glider may overtake another glider on either side. This is because when hill soaring it is only safe to make turns outwards from the hill (see page 29). The overtaking aircraft has to keep clear of the other.

Landing

The lower glider has right of way.

The law states that, notwithstanding the above rules, it is the responsibility of every pilot to take all measures to avoid a collision. This means that a pilot

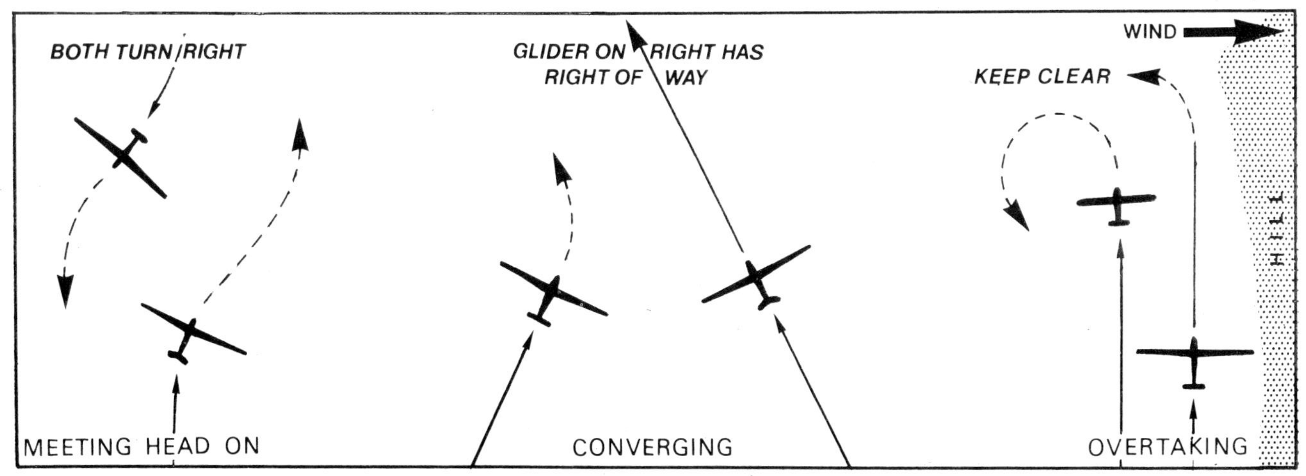

should not stand on his rights, or ever assume that the other pilot has seen him.

There are also rules for the controlled airspace around big airports and for airways, which a pilot must learn before flying cross country.

First Solo

When the instructor is satisfied that the pilot is competent to fly a circuit of the field on his own, and can cope with emergencies such as cable breaks, he will send him solo. This will normally be in the 2-seater. On some 2-seaters ballast may be needed for solo flying to keep the cockpit load within limits.

Proficiency Badges

Glider pilots in Britain do not have to hold a licence. Instead they obtain Proficiency badges. These are issued by the British Gliding Association, with the higher badges having international status. When he has successfully flown solo the new pilot can apply for his Gliding Certificate endorsed for A and B. The C follows his first soaring flight. The Bronze C, for which the pilot has to carry out 50 solo flights, 2 soaring flights of at least 30 minutes duration and pass both flying and written tests (rules of the air, meteorology, etc.), is his passport to cross-country flying. Until he has this certificate he may only fly within reach of his home field. The Silver C is the first of the international badges, and for this the pilot has to do a cross-country flight of 50 km, climb 1000 m, and make a duration flight of 5 hours. For the Gold C he has to fly a distance of 300 km and climb 3000 m. At the top there are 3 separate diamonds – distance of 500 km, a triangle or out-and-return goal flight of 300 km, and a climb of 5000 m – and the 1000 km badge for a flight exceeding this distance. There are about 50 pilots in the world who have flown 1000 km.

Barograph

If a pilot needs a record of his height for badge or record purposes he has to carry a sealed barograph. This continually records the height of the glider on a rotating drum.

Official Observers

The control and measurement of badge flights, as well as record and competition flights, is carried out by Official Observers. These are responsible volunteers appointed by the national gliding authority.

SOARING

A glider soars when it is flying in air that is rising faster than the glider is gliding down.

Most soaring and nearly all cross-country flying is done in thermals, which are large 'bubbles' of rising air. They are caused by the warming of the surface of the earth by the sun, and develop best during those hours – and months – when the sun is high in the sky. The sun warms the ground irregularly because, for example, a dry ploughed field will warm up and in turn warm the air in contact with it, more quickly than will a swamp. As the air warms its density lessens in relation to the surrounding air and it starts to rise. As it does so it expands and begins cooling. When its temperature again equals that of the surrounding air it will stop rising.

Cumulus clouds frequently form near the top of thermals, due to condensation of moisture in the rising cooling air. The height at which condensation occurs on any day is remarkably uniform, giving a flat-bottomed appearance to the cumulus clouds. They act as good signposts to the presence of thermals, but only have a short life. The average small cumulus rarely lasts longer than about 20 minutes, and for about half of its life it is decaying with no more rising air underneath. The pilot has to teach himself to recognise growing, active clouds. Good ordinary thermals are roughly 300

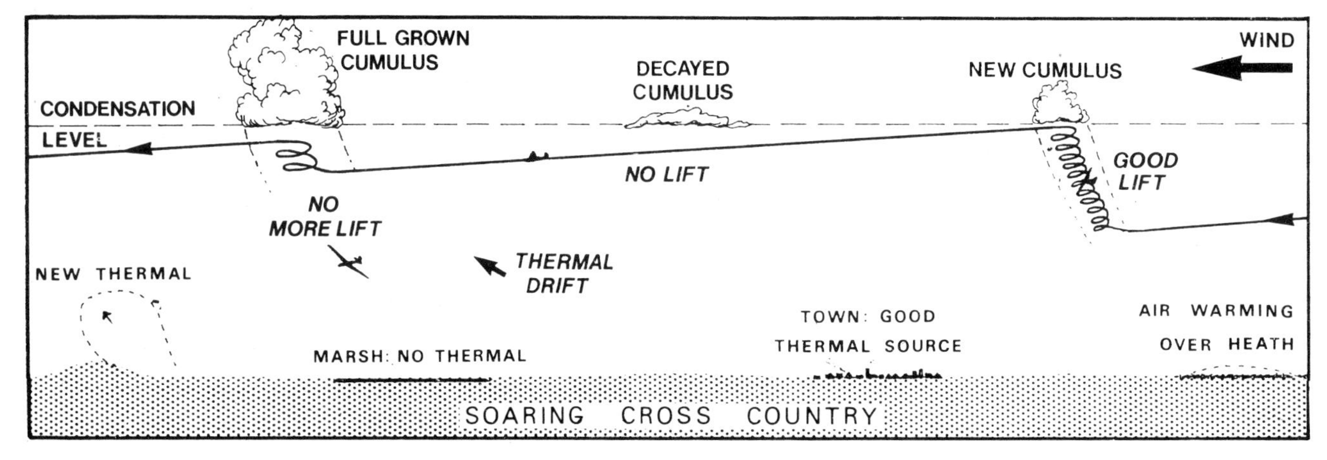

metres in diameter, about 3–6 km apart, give a net rate of climb of around 4–8 knots (400–800 ft per minute) and reach 3000–5000 ft in Britain.

As the glider flies into a thermal the variometer will first show sink as the glider passes through the air immediately surrounding the thermal, and then rise as it enters the thermal itself. The pilot will notice that the air has a sort of effervescent feel. To stay in the lift the pilot will have to circle continuously, but should wait a few seconds before starting to turn so that the glider will be in rising air all the way round the circle. It is often difficult to know whether the centre of the circle is to the left or the right, but a clue is often provided by the rising air pushing up one wing, indicating that the centre of the thermal is in that direction. The pilot should push the wing down and turn towards it.

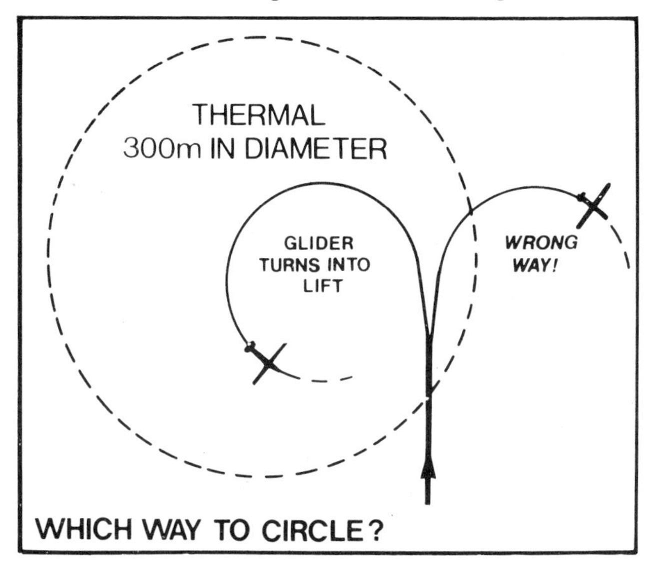

WHICH WAY TO CIRCLE?

To fly cross-country the pilot circles up within a 'bubble' of rising air, then leaves it – usually near cloud base – to fly off in the direction he has decided to go. Away from the lift he will be gliding down, losing height, so will be looking for a further thermal. He will aim for a growing cloud more or less on his course, but may, of course, run into a still newer thermal before he gets there. When he has flown around the course that he has set himself, or when he is unable to find any more lift, he lands. Should this landing have to be made in a field, it is essential that the pilot makes up his mind to stop trying to stay airborne, and concentrates on making a safe landing. On early cross-country flights the pilot should not fly at a height of less than 2000 ft above the ground over land without good fields. Down to around 1500 ft he must select a field and not allow himself to drift out of reach of it until he has selected a further suitable field. When down to 1000 ft he must concentrate on flying around the field to make a careful check of ditches, electric fences, etc., and position himself for a similar, but smaller, circuit to those he does on his home site. He should be prepared to use a lot of airbrake, even, if necessary, on the base leg, so that he will not overshoot, and then land in the normal way.

Making a field landing

The field he chooses should be large, with a long run into wind, and **must not slope downhill**. Standing crops and fields with animals should be avoided, as must fields with power or telegraph lines on the approach. The first cross-country the pilot makes will be chosen by the instructor, and will be on a day of easy thermals and good visibility. The flight will be downwind over open country to a designated easy landing field. Before departing, the pilot should explore 2 or 3 thermals within reach of base. Then, with some 3000 ft or more of height, and the sky in the direction he will be going containing plenty of growing cumulus, he should set off. On the way he should use fully all the thermals he finds, so that he will stay high. This also makes map-reading easier. It will take him about 1–2 hours to reach his destination, and with luck he will never have got so low that he had to concentrate on choosing fields. On arrival a full circuit of the landing field should be made to check wind direction and any other flying activities.

If the pilot has had the misfortune to fail to reach his goal and has come down in a field, he must first of all secure his glider with pickets or by placing his parachute in its bag on the wing tip, and then find the farmer and explain why he is there. He should leave all gates as he finds them, and do his best to keep spectators out of the field.

Pilot and crew wait for the thermals to start

Speed Flying

On early cross-country flights the pilot's concern is to complete the course, but as he does more soaring he will want to fly faster, in order to make bigger flights in the available hours of thermal activity. This he can do by teaching himself to centre quickly in the strong lift core of the thermal, by choosing only strong thermals, and by leaving them when they begin to weaken. He can also increase his cross-country speed by flying faster between thermals. The best speed at which to do this is determined by the rate at which the pilot will be able to climb up again in the next thermal. By gliding faster than his best lift to drag (L/D) speed the glider will, of course, be losing height more quickly as well as travelling faster across the countryside, but this will not matter if the pilot can climb up again in the next thermal rapidly enough to more than make up for the extra height lost when gliding fast. The MacCready ring on the variometer should be set to the strength of the thermals, so that the best speed to fly between thermals will be shown on the dial.

When thermals weaken later in the day the pilot will have to fly more slowly between them if he is to have the best chance of completing his flight. When selecting a triangular course the pilot should arrange it so that he can fly the leg which is most nearly against the wind at the time of day when thermals are strongest.

Navigation

Gliders are navigated mainly by map reading. The compass is used only as a check, because the pilot may spend as much as half – sometimes more – of the entire flight circling round and round in order to stay up. If visibility is good the relatively slow cross-country speed of a thermalling glider, plus the excellent view from the cockpit, makes navigation a relatively simple affair. It is, however, easy to get lost if insufficient attention is paid to landmarks and the glider is being flown aimlessly about while the pilot searches for lift, or when flying in poor visibility. Maps used are ICAO aeronautical charts of 1:500,000 (8 miles to the inch) and 1:250,000 (4 miles to the inch).

Cloud Flying

It is not practicable to fly out of sight of the ground without blind flying instruments and the skill to use them, because the pilot becomes disorientated and is no longer able to control his aircraft. Cloud flying should also not be carried out in or near controlled airspace. The ability to cloud fly is most useful when cumulus are large and widely separated, so that the pilot can climb high enough to reach the next source of lift. Although it is possible for the pilot to teach himself to cloud fly by entering only little clouds to begin with, it is better to obtain formal training with an instructor. There is always the risk of losing control; the glider may inadvertently be flown too fast and receive structural damage. If any speed increase becomes beyond the pilot's control he should open his airbrakes.

Slope and Wave Soaring

Slope soaring. When the wind blows against the face of a hill, it lifts up over the top. If a glider is flown back and forth along a ridge that faces the wind it will stay up. Slope soaring may be used as an end in itself or as a means of locating thermal lift to start – or continue – a cross-country flight. The glider may often be flying very low when slope soaring, sometimes below the crest of a ridge, so the pilot has to be careful not to be blown back into the hill or the turbulent air behind it. All turns should be made outwards from the hill.

Wave Soaring. When air flows over a range of mountains it will sometimes behave downwind of such obstructions rather like water does in a river down-

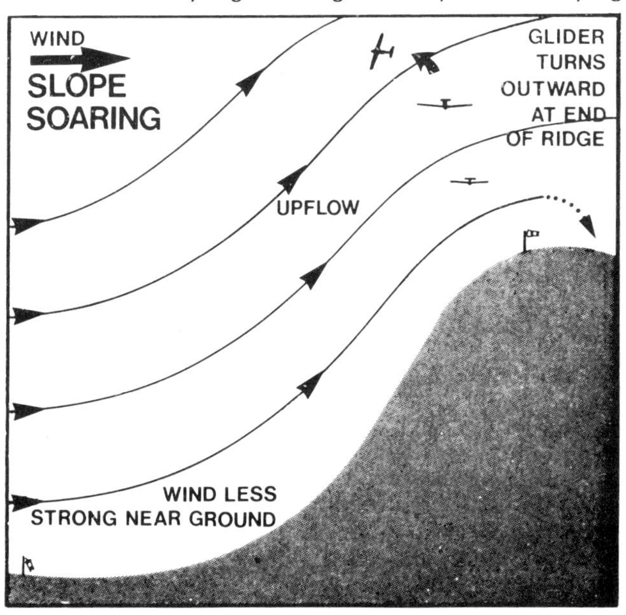

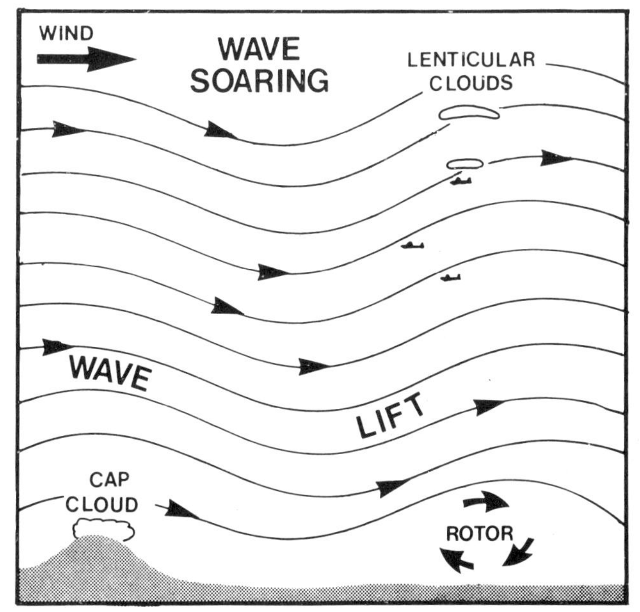

Thermal Soaring

stream of a rock. Wave-like ripples develop, except that in the air they are large, are marked by hard-edged *lenticular* clouds, and may go to great heights. The world altitude record of 46,000 ft was made in a wave. Wave soaring is best in fresh to strong winds. At height the wind is likely to be much stronger – perhaps 100 knots (185 km per hour) or more. Because the wave is caused by a mountain fixed to the ground, its wave system is also stationary. To stay in the upgoing part of the wave, therefore, the pilot also has to remain above the appropriate area of ground – perhaps 20,000 ft below him. If, at this height, the wind is 90 knots (167 km per hour) he will have to fly, heading into wind, at this speed, in order not to be blown back over the ground and into the down going part of the wave.

High altitude wave flying is a complex business. The pilot needs oxygen and should be prepared for temperatures down to −40°C, for wing and canopy icing, and for cloud to form underneath him more quickly than he is able to descend. He should also remember that it gets dark on the ground before it does high up. The sun sets 15 minutes earlier on the ground than at 10,000 ft. Landing in the dark is difficult – and for a glider maybe illegal.

Soaring Weather

The best soaring weather occurs in summer on days with strong thermal development and little or no upper cloud to reduce the heat of the sun. If the air is generally moist, cumulus will tend to overdevelop and cover the whole sky, obscuring the sun until the existing cloud decays away. If the air is unstable and the weather hot and humid, cumulus may go on growing upwards and develop into cumulo-nimbus, the clouds of thunderstorms. The lift underneath and within the cloud itself will be strong, and heights of 25–30,000 ft may be reached. Such storms are very dangerous for the unskilled pilot because of severe turbulence, icing, hail and the risk of lightning strikes.

Sea Breezes

On a day of good thermals vast quantities of air are rising over the land and this causes cooler air to be pulled in from the sea at low levels. Depending on the degree of heating this sea breeze may penetrate up to 50 km or more inland. On land covered by the cooler sea air thermals will be weaker, or non-existant, and any cumulus will be lower. Sometimes the land wind and the sea wind converge, causing a line of good up-currents, often with cumulus along the meeting zone. This is called a sea breeze front.

Weather Forecasts and Flight Planning

The best soaring weather develops when the pressure is on the high side, or at least rising, such as occurs in anticyclones, ridges of high pressure, or in the air mass following the passage of a depression. The pilot not only needs to learn about the weather, but must continually observe it, so that he becomes familiar with the appearance of the sky and can recognise its behaviour. He should be able to interpret the weather maps produced in some newspapers and on the TV, and study them for several days before any cross-country flight. Immediately prior to planning his actual course the pilot should obtain information on the direction and strength of the wind, the time thermals are likely to start and how late in the day they will continue, the estimated height of cloud base, whether conditions are right for wave or sea breeze development or thunderstorms, and whether thermals are likely to be damped by an approaching depression, broken up by increasing wind, or affected by other factors. The pilot should then work out the total distance related to the sort of speed he expects to be able to achieve, and plan a suitable triangular or out-and-return course. If he is not too sure of the weather, he could give himself a 'turn back' point to improve his chances of returning home.

Championship Flying and Records

Gliding is a sport which provides good competition flying. Each day a task is set – mostly for speed around a course several hundred kilometres in length – and the performance of each pilot is scored in proportion to the best pilot. The day winner gets 1000 points. At the end of the competition period, usually 1–2 weeks, the scores of each pilot are added together to give the final results. A pilot may do 30 hours flying, or more, in a competition. Gliders are usually divided into two, or perhaps three, Classes.

Championships scene

Launching is invariably by aerotow with the gliders releasing in a set zone. If the task is for speed, each glider has to cross a start line at a height below 1000 m, or photograph a 'ground clock', so that its time can be taken. On reaching any designated turning points the pilot has to photograph them using a cartridge camera, usually fixed inside the canopy so that the picture will show the left wing tip. The competition flight ends when the glider, identified by the contest number on the tail, is timed across a finish line.

During the flight the pilot will try to fly as fast as possible, using thermals in company with other gliders or sometimes being on his own. It is not necessary to continue to look for thermals right up to the end of the flight because at some point during the return the pilot will have enough height to reach the airfield without doing any more circling. On reaching this point the pilot can start his final glide. He will not, however, commence it the instant that he calculates he has just enough height to get over the airfield boundary fence. It is better to retain a margin of height that will enable him to fly really fast on the final glide and so save precious seconds. This margin also provides a safety factor against flying through unexpected sinking air since the pilot can reduce his own sink rate by slowing up to a more economical speed. To ease the arithmetical problem of relating speed-to-fly with actual height and distance from home the pilot uses a small calculator like a simple circular slide-rule.

Since several gliders will often be racing across the finish line at much the same time, very low and fast, the risk of collision would be high if pilots indulged in sharp turns or other exuberant manoeuvres.

Radio

Many gliders are fitted with small radio transmitters for ordinary soaring, but radio is essential for competition flying. Pilots need to inform the officials when they are approaching the start line – on a hazy day a glider is hard to see at a height of 1000 metres. If cloud flying is permitted pilots have to keep announcing their altitudes in order to be able to maintain separation from each other. They also want to keep their trailer crew informed of the glider's position and altitude so as to reduce any unnecessary car driving and to speed up the retrieve should this be needed.

The frequencies for soaring are 130.10, 130.25 and 130.40 MHz and no operator's licence is necessary when using only these frequencies or the ground-to-ground frequency of 129.9 MHz.

Water Ballast

When thermals are really strong a heavy glider will do well, but when they are weak, a lightly-loaded glider will be better. To overcome the problem of widely differing upcurrent strengths in the same flight most high performance gliders are built to carry water ballast in the wings. If, during the flight, thermals become weak, and in any case before landing, the pilot releases the water. This comes out as a fine mist trail and soon evaporates in the air. Some big competition gliders take off with as much as 200 kg of water; in a few cases the water may weigh as much as the glider itself.

Nimbus 2
Span 20.3m
Wing area 14.4m²
Aspect ratio 28.6
Weight empty 340 kg
Flying weight 530 kg (including ballast)
Best glide ratio 49:1
Minimum sink 0.48 m/sec

LOOKING AFTER YOUR GLIDER

A glider pilot not only needs to be able to fly, soar, navigate and understand the weather, he has to be able to rig and de-rig his glider and generally look after it. Most gliders have a trailer so that they can be retrieved from fields, and this has to be cared for as well.

Glider cockpits are designed for a pilot wearing a parachute. Even though he may never have to use it to save his life, the parachute should always be in good condition and be worn properly adjusted. It should be professionally re-packed at intervals, and should not be allowed to get wet or be contaminated by oil, etc.

Most privately-owned gliders are owned by a group or syndicate of pilots, usually 3 or 4. This not only reduces the cost, but deals with the problem of helpers for rigging or retrieving. When joining a syndicate the pilot should make clear arrangements about insurance, who pays what, and who flies when. Syndicate ownership is probably the best way to get a lot of good flying.

Rigging and De-rigging

To go in its trailer the glider has to be taken apart; the wings, for example, divide into 2 or 3 pieces. Before flight it has to be put together again, and this must be done so that the wings or other fittings are not strained during assembly, and are properly secured. It is not difficult, but it must be done conscientiously; helpers must know what to do, and the assembled glider must be carefully inspected.

Even if the glider is kept in a hangar it must be given a pre-flight check each day before flying, and must be signed for by the pilot doing the inspection. It should also be thoroughly examined after a heavy landing. At intervals, usually once a year, the glider is given a thorough overhaul for renewal of its certificate of airworthiness. It goes without saying that the glider should be kept clean and polished, particularly the wings and the canopy.

Polishing and preparing for flight

INFORMATION

Costs

Gliding is not a particularly cheap sport, and because it takes considerable enthusiasm and effort to become a good pilot, it is usually sensible to start with a trial flight and then a week's basic course. The cost of this is comparable with similar holiday weeks in other sports, and it gives enough opportunity for a person to know whether he wants to go on or not. If he does continue the new pilot must be prepared to part with time as well as money, but his first solo, first cross-country flight, and first competition will become highlights in his life.

The Fédération Aeronautique Internationale

The FAI is the international authority for all sporting flying, and through its technical commissions (the gliding one is CIVV, from its title in French) determines the rules for World Championships, Records and International Proficiency badges. There are categories of Records for single-seater and two-seaters, and for speed around triangular courses, or out and returns, and for distance and altitude. In its own country the national Gliding Association can modify or add to the FAI Sporting Code rules for national or local records or competitions.

The British Gliding Association

The British Gliding Association, Kimberley House, Vaughan Way, Leicester, is the national authority for gliding in Great Britain. It is a member of the Royal Aero Club of the United Kingdom, which is in turn a member of the FAI.

The BGA operates through an elected Executive Committee, with various specialist committees, and a secretariat.

The following services and information are available:

Standards and application forms for pilot proficiency badges, official observer, instructor rating, certification of airworthiness, approved glider inspectors, as well as lists of gliding clubs, pilot training courses, and various sales items.

Its magazine *Sailplane and Gliding* is published every second month and is available through the BGA or on order from newsagents.

Further Reading

Complete Hang Gliding Guide Noel Whittall (A & C Black)
Complete Soaring Guide Ann Welch (A & C Black)
Pilots Weather Ann Welch (John Murray)

INDEX